CONTENTS

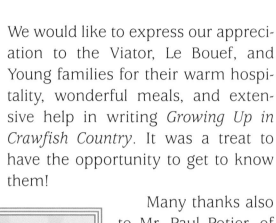

ACKNOWLEDGMENTS

We would like to express our appreciation to the Viator, Le Bouef, and Young families for their warm hospitality, wonderful meals, and extensive help in writing *Growing Up in Crawfish Country*. It was a treat to have the opportunity to get to know them!

Many thanks also to Mr. Paul Potier, of Potier's Prairie Cajun Inn & Gifts, and Ms. Debbie Richard, of the Eunice Chamber of Commerce, for introducing us to Alida, Jared, and Meghann. Finally, we are very grateful to Ms. Olive Seale Gill for permission to include her painting, *A Cajun Mardi Gras*, in this book.

K.G.
S.D.

In many ways, people in the United States are very similar to one another. We all listen to the same music, watch the same movies and television programs, eat the same burgers, French fries, and pizza, and wear the same clothes.

But if you look closer, you'll see that Americans are different from each other too. Not only do we have traits that make each of us unique individuals, but we often have different cultural characteristics that identify us as belonging to a particular ethnic, religious, or racial group.

Generally, the longer a particular group of people live in this country and interact with other Americans, the more they become like everyone else. Thus, after a few generations, most immigrants retain relatively little of their original cultures.

However, some groups have been in this country for hundreds of years, yet have kept alive the cultures of their ancestors. In most ways, they live just like other Americans. But, at the same time, they have preserved their own special traditions, religious

ABOUT GROWING UP IN AMERICA

beliefs, music, foods, ways of talking, and sometimes even their own languages.

Some of these groups came from Europe or Africa, while others are Native Americans who have been here all along. But all have made important contributions to the way Americans live and to the common culture that we share. I thought you might like to meet some children from these different cultures and learn about their lives, so I decided to write this series to introduce them to you.

If you've ever had Cajun food, you know a little bit about the culture of the children in this book. Although most Americans have only recently begun enjoying blackened catfish and other Cajun dishes, the Cajun people of southwestern Louisiana have been eating these foods for a very long time. But there are many things besides food that make the Cajun people and their culture special. For example, some Cajuns still speak a unique type of French that their ancestors brought with them from Nova Scotia—their first settlement in North America—two hundred years ago.

My friend, Sylviane, comes from France, so of course, she speaks French too. A few years ago, Sylviane visited Eunice, Louisiana. She thought it would be the perfect place to find some Cajun children you might like to know. Since it's always more fun to do things with a friend, we decided to write this book together. We think you'll really like Alida, Jared, and Meghann—three Cajun children we met in Eunice.

K.G.

ALIDA, JARED, AND MEGHANN

It's a hot, steamy day, but twelve-year-old Alida (Ah-lee-DAH) Viator is wearing two long-sleeved shirts. Her jeans are tucked into a pair of heavy leather boots, and she has a big bandanna tied over her forehead and hair.

This may seem like a lot of clothes to be wearing in 95 degree weather, but Alida is going to need them. She and her dog, **Pistache,** are on their way to her favorite place—the **bayou** that runs alongside her family's farm. A bayou is a swampy river or stream in southern Louisiana. Like most bayous, this one is loaded with mosquitoes.

"I'd rather be too hot," Alida says, laughing, "than be eaten alive." Her shirts, jeans, and bandanna help protect her from mosquitoes, but the

Lots of clothes and heavy boots help protect Alida from mosquitoes and snakes.

Cypress and other trees grow so closely together that it's difficult to walk along the bayou.

boots have another purpose. "You can't walk in all this mud without them," she says.

Also, mosquitoes aren't the only things in a bayou that bite. There are poisonous copperhead and cottonmouth snakes to watch out for, too. "Thick boots are a big help around snakes," Alida adds. "They can't bite through the leather."

Like many people in southwestern Louisiana, Alida loves the slow, murky bayous that meander through the country-side. Her family and others like them have made their homes alongside these waterways for over two hundred years, and it's

Prairies surround the bayous around Eunice, Louisiana, Alida's hometown.

no surprise that she's comfortable there. Nevertheless, it's easy to get lost exploring the thick woods that line the shore, so Alida takes a compass with her.

Alida and most of the folks in her community are Cajuns. They are the descendants of French settlers who came to Louisiana in the middle and late 1700s, after being pushed out of Nova Scotia, Canada, by the British. Since the French name for Nova Scotia was Acadie, these settlers were called Acadians. With time, Acadian was shortened to Cajun. Until very recently, most Cajuns still spoke a type of French. And even now, Cajuns have a very special culture that is all their own.

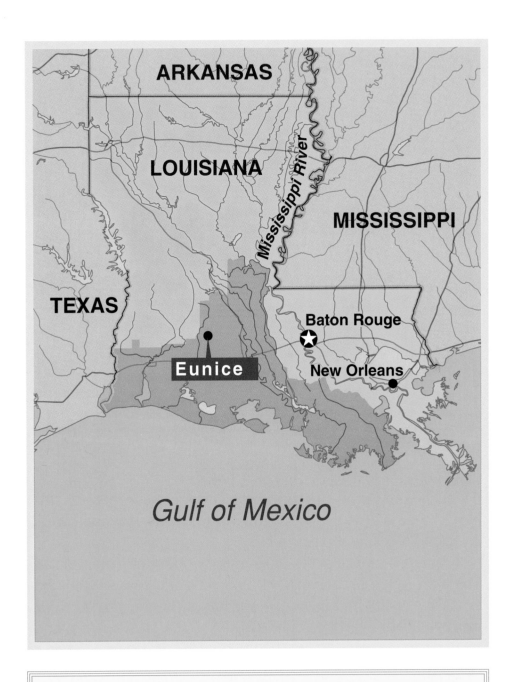

Today, Cajuns still live primarily in the parts of Louisiana (shaded area) settled by their Acadian ancestors.

FROM ACADIE TO LOUISIANA

During the long struggle between the French and the English for control of North America, the French colonists of Acadie found themselves in a difficult position. Their land had changed hands between England and France ten times between 1604 and 1710. Since they could never be sure which their next ruler would be, the Acadians tried to avoid taking sides. When the British gained final possession of Acadie in 1713, renaming it Nova Scotia, the Acadians were unwilling to take an oath of loyalty to England, but they promised not to aid the French.

The Acadians kept their promise. Nevertheless, their presence made the British government of Nova Scotia nervous. Worried that their French-speaking subjects might not stay neutral, the English came up with a plan to solve this troublesome situation—they would simply get rid of the Acadians.

In 1755, the British tricked four hundred Acadian men into going to a meeting, where they were all arrested. With the men safely under lock and key, their families were told to report for deportation. Then men, women, and children were loaded into waiting boats and shipped away.

Soon the people in other Acadian communities were also deported. By 1760, about six thousand Acadians out of a total of twelve thousand to eighteen thousand had been forced to leave. Those who escaped deportation fled to Quebec or nearby areas still controlled by the French.

The ships carrying the Acadians were ordered to distribute their captives among the English colonies to the south, from

Loaded onto unsanitary ships and given little food, the Acadians were sent into exile.

Massachusetts to Georgia. By spreading the Acadians down the Atlantic coast, the English hoped to force them to adopt the culture of the British settlers and keep them from helping the French.

The plan was a disaster. Crowded into small, dark ships and given little food and water, the Acadians became weak and sick. Typhoid and smallpox broke out killing many. This treatment made the Acadians very angry. They were determined to not become part of English colonial society and resisted the efforts to separate them from each other.

The British settlers were also unhappy with the situation. In the middle of their war against the French and the Indians, the last thing the English colonists wanted was to have enemy people living among them. In addition, the French-speaking Acadians were Catholic, while most British colonists were Protestant. This added to the mistrust and dislike the English felt.

Some colonies, such as Virginia and New Jersey, refused to accept any Acadians and ordered them sent on to England. There the Acadians were forced to wait out the war in prison camps, where half of them died in epidemics.

Other colonies allowed the Acadians in, but did little to help them. The government in England set aside no money for the Acadians' support. The Acadians were farmers, but without land or farm equipment, they had no way to earn a living. Therefore, the English settlers were taxed to provide for their new neighbors. This increased the resentment and anger they felt toward the Acadians. In this hostile environment, many of the Acadians died, while the rest were barely able to survive.

Unfortunately, the treatment given Acadian exiles in France was little better. As farmers, they expected the French government to give them land where they could build homes and raise crops. Instead, they were dumped in coastal cities and abandoned by the government. Since they lacked the skills to find jobs in the cities, they—like most Acadians elsewhere—slipped into lives of poverty.

By the end of the French and Indian War in 1763, Acadians throughout North America and Europe were eager to leave their miserable living conditions and find a place where they could reestablish their way of life and reunite their community. Two thousand were lured to the French colony of Saint-Domingue, now Haiti, by a false promise of fertile farmland if they helped build a naval base on the island. Most of these people died, while many of the survivors ended up poverty stricken.

As part of the 1763 treaty that ended the war between France and England, Louisiana was given to Spain. A year later, a handful of Acadians migrated there and settled along the Mississippi River. Then in 1765, two hundred Acadians from detention camps in Nova Scotia followed and established farms on the western frontier. News of the opportunities offered in Louisiana soon spread among Acadian exiles in Maryland and Pennsylvania, and they started migrating in large numbers as well.

Although the relationship between the Spanish colonial government and the Acadians was sometimes rocky, this time the Acadians were in luck—the Spanish needed them as much as they needed Louisiana. The colony of Louisiana was sparsely populated and the Spanish were anxious to fill it with settlers. The hard-working Acadians succeeded in turning the land into productive farms and this impressed the new government. Meanwhile, encouraging letters from Louisiana had made the Acadians in France eager to come to the colony. Most, however, did not have the money to make the trip. This problem was solved when the Spanish government offered to transport the Acadians for free. Thus, in 1785, two thousand Acadians left France to join their friends and relatives in Louisiana.

At last, the long journey of the Acadians was over. It had taken thirty years, but they had finally found what they had been looking for—a place where they could live together and a home they could call their own.

Traditionally, most Cajuns lived on small farms. Alida's family still does. She, her older brother, Moïse (Mo-EEZ), and her mom and dad raise workhorses. But it's hard to support a family from farm earnings alone, so Alida's dad has another job in New Orleans during the week. Since New Orleans is 150 miles away, he lives there from Monday to Friday. Then on Friday night, he drives home for the weekend and does the heavy jobs around the farm.

Living on a farm means lots of work for everyone. This is one reason why Alida and Moïse do not attend regular school. Most children in Eunice go to public or parochial schools. But Alida and her brother are taught at home by their mother.

It's up to Alida and Moïse to decide when to do their chores and when to study. "Some days, I work more outside,"

It's Alida's job to groom **Beau Fou,** the farm's stud colt.

Alida says. "I mow the lawn, garden, haul trees, things like that. Then I have to make up school the next day."

Alida and Moïse also decide on their own grades. While it's tempting, they don't always give themselves A's. "They're both painfully honest," Alida's mom says. "I've never had either one of them give themselves a grade they didn't deserve."

16

Going to school at home means that Alida and Moïse don't get to hang out much with other kids. But there are children around to do things with. "We still have friends that we met when we went to public school a few years ago," Alida says. "And there's a neighbor who's twelve who lives right across the bayou, and he's home schooled too."

Most of Alida's time is spent with her family. There is a lake on the farm where she and Moïse often fish. Fishing is relaxing and fun, and fresh fish make a great dinner.

Alida and her brother are busy doing other things too. Like their parents, both are musicians, and they need lots of time to practice. They also need to be free to travel when they are invited to perform out of town. In addition, the family makes violins to sell, and that requires time.

Alida decided she wanted to play the violin when she was very young—and from the beginning, she knew just who she wanted to teach her. "Around here, we have a lot of big community dances. It's a family activity where grandparents, teenagers, and little kids all dance with each other. She was about

Alida's classroom is in her bedroom, and her mother is her teacher.

The lake is just a short distance from the bayou, but the two look very different.

After they catch the fish, Alida and Moïse have to clean them.

seven when she started going with us," Alida's mom recalls. "At one of these dances, she heard Steve Riley and the Mamou Playboys, a local Cajun group. Well, she fixed her mind on the fiddle player in the group—that he was the one who was going to teach her to play the fiddle. She nagged me until she got me to talk to him. He said he didn't teach, and he especially didn't teach kids."

Alida's mom thought that would be the end of it, but Alida had no intention of giving up. "We saw him playing another time, and she said, 'Mama, Mama, go over and talk to him,'" her mom continues. "So I did, and he said no again. This went on for about three months."

The fiddler finally relented when Alida went up and asked him herself. "I introduced myself to him and said, 'my name is Alida'—that's a name that's in Cajun songs. And he said, 'Well, if your name is Alida, I guess I can't refuse.'"

Alida took lessons from him for two years. "He was a great teacher!" she says. "He separated each song bit by bit and showed me every single note." Alida still does not read

"Alida was doing the fiddle, my mom likes the bass, and my dad plays the accordion, the harmonica, and the drums," Moïse says, "so I chose the guitar."

Alida was six or seven when this picture was taken—around the age when she started taking fiddle lessons. Moïse, then about nine years old, is playing the rub board in the background, and their father is singing at the microphone.

music. Instead, she learns a song by listening to it. If she thinks it would sound better if played a little differently, she improvises.

Alida was just as persistent with Mr. Ortego, the man who taught the Viators how to make fiddles. "He said he wasn't making fiddles anymore," her mom says, "but Alida was determined that he was going to do it."

It takes the Viators about two hundred hours—or a month and a half to two months—to make a violin. "Everyone works on different pieces at different times," Alida explains. "I think

Moïse would rather work on one piece at a time, so he can say, 'I made that.' But I like to jump around from part to part."

The top of a fiddle starts out as a flat piece of wood. The shape is drawn on the wood and cut out. Next, the top is carved so that the center part curves up. When the top has been carved and sanded down so that it's thin enough, two F-shaped holes are cut out. These holes allow sound to resonate inside the violin.

The one thing that the family doesn't make is the bow. "We made one," Alida says, "but they're pretty boring to do." Also, there isn't as much of a market for bows. "Fiddle players may have five to ten fiddles, but they usually have only one or two bows that they use on all of them," she explains.

Alida enjoys experimenting with different colors on the fiddles. The one she's working on now is going to be stained green. Each fiddle also has a different design carved on the end of the neck. Carving the neck is the most difficult part of making a fiddle, so Alida's mom does that.

After working for so long on an

It took some persuading to get Mr. Ortego to teach the Viators how to make violins, but Alida finally convinced him they were serious.

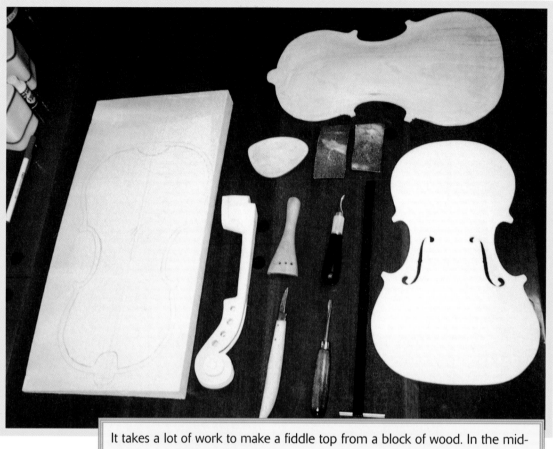

It takes a lot of work to make a fiddle top from a block of wood. In the middle are the fiddle neck, the chin rest, and some of the tools the Viators use.

instrument, it can be hard to part with it. As Alida comments, "Every fiddle we make, we say, 'I don't want to sell this one. This is my favorite!'"

There are plenty of potential customers around for the Viators' fiddles. Music has always been a very important part of Cajun life, and sometimes it seems as if almost everyone in Eunice is a musician. On Saturdays, folks crowd into a local ac-

At this stage, the wood is very thin, and Alida has to be careful not to sand a hole right through it.

cordion shop to play Cajun songs. People of all ages bring their instruments—fiddles, guitars, accordions, bass guitars, *le 'tit fer* (triangles), and ***cuillères*** (spoons)—and just join in. Since many can play more than one instrument, they often trade with each other after a few songs.

Cajuns are famous for their love of music, dancing, and having a good time, and this is especially true during ***Mardi Gras***.

23

These are a few of the fiddles Alida and her family have made.

Mardi Gras means "Fat Tuesday," and it is a Catholic holiday celebrated each year on the day before Ash Wednesday. (In addition to being the name of the holiday, Mardi Gras also refers to anyone who takes part in the celebration.) Ash Wednesday marks the beginning of Lent, the forty-day period leading up to Easter. Lent is a time of fasting and repentance, so traditionally, Catholics do not have parties, dances, or festivals then.

24

CAJUN MUSIC

When the Acadians went to
Louisiana, they took with them the
violin, or fiddle, and the peasant
folk songs, ballads, drinking songs,
and sea chanties that they had
originally sung in France. But once
in Louisiana, their music began to
change.

From their Spanish neighbors,
the Cajuns borrowed the guitar. As
Cajun music began to absorb the
sounds of country and western
songs from Texas, the guitar became more and more important.
The melody of one of the most
popular Cajun songs, "J'ai Passe
Devant Ta Porte" (I Passed By Your
Door) came from a Spanish ballad.

African Americans also helped shape
Cajun music. The bluesy sound of
Southern black music was incorporated

There are other types of accordions
used in Louisiana, but Alida's father
and other Cajun musicians play only
the Cajun, or single-row button
accordion.

into Cajun singing, changing French ditties into mournful
songs. Cajuns adopted African percussion techniques,
using scrap metal and household items such as spoons
and washboards, to keep the beat. One of the most
famous Cajun musicians, Amede Ardoin, was a black man.

Cajun music owes much of its distinctive sound to

German settlers who introduced the accordion to southwestern Louisiana in the 1880s. Alida's father plays both the Cajun accordion and the harmonica. He describes the similarities between the two in this way: "The original accordion invented in Germany has some of the notes of the full European scale missing, so it's tuned just like the blues harmonica. By a weird coincidence, the West African blues scale fits the scale of the original German button accordion and the harmonica. That's why they sound so good together. It's also one reason why Cajun music sounds so bluesy."

It's very hard to describe Cajun music because it's unique. It sounds a little like country and western, a little like Appalachian bluegrass, and a little like blues—but it's different from all of them. If you'd like to hear this music for yourself, there are some Cajun albums suggested in "More About Cajuns" at the end of this book.

The majority of Cajuns, including the three families in this book, are Catholics. Thus, Mardi Gras is the last chance for most folks to really enjoy themselves before Easter, and they make the most of the opportunity. Celebrations start the Saturday before and reach a height on Fat Tuesday.

Cajun Mardi Gras is different from the Mardi Gras celebration in New Orleans. In Cajun country, a big part of the holiday is the Mardi Gras Run. In towns throughout southwestern Louisiana, men dressed in Mardi Gras masks and costumes

In this painting of the Mardi Gras Run by an artist from Eunice, men disguised in costumes leave a farm where the family gave them a chicken. The captain of the run always wears a hat and a cape.

meet in the early morning hours and set out on horseback to visit farms in the area. At each house, they ask the farmers for gifts of food, such as a chicken or rice. Then they bring everything they collect back to town where it's made into a big **gumbo** and shared with everyone in the community.

Last year, for the first time, the town of Eunice had a children's run. Because he wrote the winning essay in a contest on what Mardi Gras means, ten-year-old Jared Le Bouef was chosen to be the captain. As he said in his essay, "Mardi Gras to me means keeping alive the traditions and customs that make us special as people of southern Louisiana." He added,

27

Traditionally, the run is on horseback, but after this picture was taken, Jared rode a three-wheeler the rest of the way.

"I would love the chance to act as a co-captain of the Mardi Gras. This would be a dream come true."

The experience was every bit as exciting as he had imagined! Dressed in their costumes, over three hundred children paraded around the center of town, led by Jared on a three-wheeler. "Everybody wanted to know how I got to be the one to ride the three-wheeler [an all-terrain vehicle]," Jared said. "When they saw me doing that, a lot of them wanted to do it too."

As in Mardi Gras parades throughout Louisiana, the children threw strings of beads to onlookers. "The kids run after those beads like they were a million dollars," Jared's dad says, "trying to get the prettiest ones."

After the walking parade, the children and some parents climbed into cars or aboard flatbed trucks and trailers and took off for the countryside. Everything was fine until they reached the first farm. The youngsters went up to the house and asked if they could have a chicken. The family said yes and, as is customary, they gave the children a live bird.

"Jared was supposed to hold the chicken by its legs and throw it in the air," his mom said. "Then all the other kids try to grab the poor little thing. The one who catches it is considered an outstanding Mardi Gras."

"But when I threw the chicken up, it ran back toward me," Jared recalls.

"The kids took off running after the chicken, and Jared got trampled," his dad adds. "They knocked him flat! They even knocked down some mothers. They were determined to catch that bird!" After that experience, Jared decided that someone else could throw the next chicken.

It's no wonder that Jared likes Mardi Gras so much. His family has always been very involved in celebrat-

Jared leads the children's Mardi Gras parade around town, as other kids and his mom follow.

29

The rest of the year, Jared spends most of his free time playing sports. His father's employer sponsors his baseball team, and his dad is one of the coaches.

Jared shoots some hoops in front of his house with his dad and a few friends.

ing this holiday. Since he was little, Jared has gone with his grandparents to watch the adult Mardi Gras Run. And his grandmother has been making the family's Mardi Gras costumes for years. As the children get bigger, she adds material onto the bottom. Mardi Gras costumes are supposed to be a bit raggedy, so it doesn't matter if they don't fit perfectly.

Although Mardi Gras is basically the same in all the neighboring towns, each place adds its own distinctive style. "Right down the road, in Iota, the costumes are the same, but the

Jared's grandmother (in the middle with his grandfather) made these Mardi Gras costumes.

masks are different," Jared explains. "Their masks have long, pointy noses." The long ugly nose is the sign of the villain, a traditional character.

In some towns, people dress in burlap sacks, and in nearby Hathaway, the masks are painted black. Eunice's style is to use the traditional New Orleans Mardi Gras colors—green, purple, and gold. Green stands for faith, purple for justice, and gold for power.

The hat and the mask are important parts of the costume.

31

The costumes Jared, his cousin, and his little sister wear are in traditional Mardi Gras colors. They made their masks by painting faces on wire screens.

Mardi Gras hats originated long ago in medieval France. In those days, peasants took advantage of the celebration to make fun of the rich and powerful by dressing in hats that represented the upper classes. The bishop's hat stood for the officials of the Catholic Church. The mortarboard, or graduation hat, represented the educated people. The tall, pointed hats worn by royal women symbolized the aristocracy. Mortarboards and bishops' hats are still worn during Mardi Gras in some Cajun towns, but the tall, pointed hats, called **capuchons**, are traditional in Eunice. Jared's mom is a third-grade teacher, and she sometimes helps children make their capuchons in class.

The masks are made of wire screens with faces painted on them. With these masks on, it's difficult to recognize anyone—even a friend. As Jared's mom says, "The adults get dressed in these costumes and act really crazy, pinching people and things. You don't know who they are—even if it's someone

Masks with pointed noses are from the neighboring town of Iota, or "Ti Mamou" (Little Mamou).

It's a real honor to win Best All-Around Mardi Gras, so Meghann is very proud of her trophy.

you know really well. Everybody's hair is pushed back, so only the eyes and mouth show. Sometimes, they won't say anything because they don't want you to recognize the voice."

Prizes are given out at the children's walking parade for the best costumes and for the best overall Mardi Gras participant. The more fringe a costume has and the more work that went into making it, the better it's judged to be. But to win best overall Mardi Gras, a child must do the things traditionally associated with the celebration, and that means dancing a lot. Many children have little bells sewn on their costumes so you can hear them when they dance.

Last year, the prize for outstanding female Mardi Gras went to ten-year-old Meghann Young. "My friends and I went around and begged for money," Meghann says. "I think that's mostly what got me the trophy for all-around female Mardi Gras. I've always seen the men running Mardi Gras begging for money for the gumbo, so that's where I got the idea."

"You have to entertain the crowd, that's part of being a good Mardi Gras," her mom adds. "You get your money by dancing—to help pay for the meat in the gumbo."

Her dad thinks Meghann is a typical Cajun in other ways as well. "One of the things that makes her a good Cajun is that she loves to hunt and fish," he says. Although Meghann has an older sister and brother, she's the one who's most likely to accompany her father. "She's my partner," her dad adds. "Most little girls don't get into it that much, but we hunt dove, squirrel, rabbit, deer, and ducks. Her favorite food is wild game—she loves that!"

"I know some people are antihunting," Meghann's father continues, "but we don't just go out and shoot things. Anything we kill is something that we're going to eat. Nothing is wasted."

"I never shoot anything," Meghann says, "but it's fun to go out there. And it feels good to know how to use the gun at least." What Meghann enjoys most of all is fishing. She and her dad once caught a six-pound catfish.

"And, boy, I'll tell you—Meghann loves to eat!" her dad says, laughing. Luckily for her, Meghann's father is considered one of the best cooks in town. And that's saying a lot, since

Although she hasn't shot any animals, Meghann has learned to use a gun.

WHO ARE THE CAJUNS?

As Meghann says, "Most of us can probably trace back somewhere to the people who were deported from Canada." But the Acadians have changed a lot since they first arrived in Louisiana. It is these changes—as well as their Acadian ancestry—that make Alida, Jared, and Meghann Cajuns.

Perhaps the most important thing that happened to the Acadians was that they met other groups who lived in Louisiana. Some Acadians married people from these other groups. As a result, the Cajuns are now a mix of ethnic groups. You can get an idea of some of the nationalities that make up the Cajun people from the last names of Alida Viator, Jared Le Bouef, and Meghann Young.

One group that the Acadians intermarried with was the Spanish. Spanish settlers were in Louisiana even before the French turned the colony over to Spain in 1763. "My father's family on his mother's side are the Manuels," Alida explains. "They settled in New Orleans—maybe in the 1730s. Pedro Manuel came to Opelousas, a nearby town, in 1782 when it was a Spanish possession. Every Manuel in this area—and there are thousands—are related to that man." The other side of her father's family also came from Spain. "The Viators came in the 1780s, too, from Malaga, Spain, " Alida adds. "Their name was Villatoro." Over the years, the name was shortened to the more French-sounding Viator.

You can see Jared's Acadian ancestry in his French last name, Le Bouef. Although their name may originally have been Le Boeuf, Jared's family now spells it Le Bouef. But many of his mother's ancestors were German. The Germans began arriving in large numbers in Louisiana in 1720, and today there are many Cajuns of German descent living in the Eunice area.

When the United States bought Louisiana in 1803, English-speaking American settlers began to flood in. Some married into Meghann's family. "My grandfather has a family tree, and you can trace our ancestors way back to France," she says. "But my great-grandmother was a McGee, and that's Irish." Like Jared, Meghann also has a lot of German in her background.

Although the Acadian culture was influenced by other people, Acadians were the largest European group in southwestern Louisiana. French was the primary language in the area, so everyone else learned to speak it. They also adopted the culture of the Acadians. In time, many forgot they weren't originally of French descent.

"My grandmother lived with us," Meghann's father recalls, "and she spoke French. She and her sister spoke no English. They were from Germany, and spoke German. But when they came to this area, everyone spoke French so they did, too."

Alida's family has a similar story. "The Manuels didn't think of themselves as Spanish," her mother says. "They just saw themselves as French like everybody else."

In the past, a person had to speak Cajun French to be considered a Cajun. Now, most Cajuns feel that a person who was born and raised in a Cajun community is a Cajun. As Meghann's father sums it up, "It's as much your culture as your ancestors that determines whether you're a Cajun."

Europeans were not the only people Acadians encountered in Louisiana. In addition to Native Americans, there were a large number of slaves and free people of African or mixed descent. These African Americans had an important influence on Acadian culture, particularly in terms of music. They also spoke French, and some Acadians and African Americans intermarried. However, today African Americans with Acadian or other French ancestry refer to themselves and the type of French that they speak as Creole, not Cajun.

Even some Native Americans in southern Louisiana still speak French. In his job as a social-service worker, Meghann's father has met Native Americans from as far away as Houma and Thibodaux who speak Cajun.

southern Louisiana is famous for its great food. "Every year, we have a World Championship Crawfish *Étouffée* Cook-off here," Meghann says proudly. "The first time they cooked, my parents won. And my grandfather won three times."

One of the most interesting traditions associated with Cajun food is the **boucherie**, or butchering. The name might sound gruesome, but it's actually a big party that combines hard work, socializing, and lots of eating. Meghann's father usually gets asked to do the cooking.

"You get everybody from the neighborhood to come over and help," Meghann says. "Sometimes, they might kill two or three hogs for butchering. Every part of the pig is used. We don't waste anything!"

Meghann gets the yucky job of cleaning out the intestines.

Much of the pig meat is made into sausage, which is smoked and stored. The hocks are salted down, and the lard is rendered and used to store the meat. The internal organs are ground for **boudin,** a Cajun sausage made of highly seasoned pork and rice. Sometimes, even the stomach is cleaned, stuffed with seasoned meat, and smoked.

"Everybody has a certain job," Meghann's dad explains. "Meghann and I help my father make the boudin, somebody else makes the **crackling**. We had a tradition for several years—I was the one who killed the hogs. Now, my son has inherited that job."

Meghann thinks her task is the messiest of all. "In the last two boucheries, Alida and I got to clean the pig intestines," she recalls. "You take one end of the intestines and pour water through to wash out all the stuff inside. It's really gross! When the water comes out clean, then you know everything is out." The clean intestines are then used as a casing for boudin.

"Next, you take the meat and put it in a big pot and grind it up," she continues. "The grinder has a

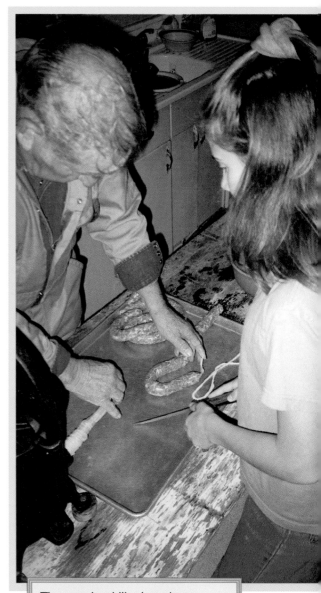

The spaghetti-like intestines are used as casing for boudin. They expand when Meghann and her grandfather fill them with meat.

39

tube where the meat comes out. You squish the intestines onto the end of this tube, and the meat goes right in."

A boucherie is not all work. There's always a band playing music, and there is time to talk with friends and neighbors. And there is tons of food to eat! In addition to the hog meat being cooked, everyone brings a dish for the potluck supper.

PAIN PERDU

Pain perdu (PAN-pair-doo)—lost bread—is a favorite in Cajun Louisiana. In the days before refrigerators, bread became stale, or "lost," very quickly. Instead of throwing it out, Cajuns turned it into a delicious dish. You'll need:

1 cup sugar
1 cup milk
2 eggs
1 teaspoon cinnamon
6 slices of day-old bread
3 tablespoons of cooking oil
powdered sugar
syrup

Mix the sugar, milk, eggs, and cinnamon throughly until the mixture is smooth. Then soak the bread slices in the mixture. Heat the oil in a skillet and fry the bread slices on both sides until they are light brown. Sprinkle the bread with powdered sugar and serve with syrup.

MR. YOUNG'S FRESH CORN "MAQUE CHOUX"

Meghann's family loves her dad's maque choux (MOCK-shoo), and you will too! You'll need the following ingredients:

1 medium onion, peeled
1 green pepper
1 medium tomato, peeled
8 ears of corn
  (or a 1-pound bag of frozen corn kernels)
1/2 cup of cooking oil
salt and pepper

To begin, chop the onion, green pepper, and tomato into small pieces. Next, husk the ears of corn thoroughly; then cut the kernels from the cob lengthwise. After removing the kernels, scrape the cob to get the juice. (Of course, if you're using frozen corn, you can skip these steps. But maque choux made with frozen corn doesn't taste quite the same.) Mix all these ingredients together in a bowl.

Heat the oil in a pot and add the mixed ingredients. Turn the heat down to low and stir. Add salt and pepper until it tastes the way you want it to. Cover the pot and cook for 45 minutes, stirring occasionally.

If you want a spicier version, you can use a small can of Rotel tomatoes instead of fresh tomato.

long with their meat and fish, folks in southwestern Louisiana eat a lot of rice. In part, that's because the land and climate there are perfect for growing it. And most Cajun food tastes delicious over rice.

Jared's uncle is a rice farmer. "Rice needs a lot of water to grow in," Jared's mom says. "In the spring, when the floods come, farmers trap the water in the rice fields with **levees**, or water the fields with underground irrigation. At the end of July, or the beginning of August, my brother takes Jared and the other boys and they load the trucks full of rice and come in to weigh it."

Rice isn't the only thing in a rice field. Crawfish—the most famous of all Cajun food—are found there as well. Crawfish look

This old-fashioned rice huller was used to remove the hard outer covering of the rice grain.

like tiny lobsters. But while lobsters live in the sea, crawfish like freshwater. And they find flooded rice fields to be just right.

From October through mid-June, people set baited cages in the water to trap the crawfish. Then they cook them in a variety of ways to make some of the most delicious meals anywhere.

Boucheries, the Mardi Gras Run, fiddle music, and foods such as boudin, gumbo, rice, and crawfish are important parts of being Cajun. But until about fifty years ago, the French language was the central feature of Cajun culture. Today, most young people in southwestern Louisiana no longer speak French. Fortunately, the language is beginning to come back.

Cajun French differs from the standard French now spoken in France and Canada. As Alida explains, "What happened was that in France, the language changed, while the language here kind of came to a stop." Thus, Cajun French still has some of the characteristics of the rural French that was spoken in medieval times in west-central France. In addition, Cajuns borrowed some words from their Native American, African, Spanish, and English neighbors. These words are not found in standard French.

Cajun was spoken by just about everyone in Eunice two generations ago, but Alida, Jared, Meghann, and most other children their age did not grow up speaking it. "My grandfather and the other kids back then would get punished by their teachers if they talked French in school, even to themselves," Jared says. "And if you spoke French, people thought you were ignorant," Meghann adds.

So children were discouraged from speaking Cajun, and the language began to die out. While many folks in their thirties or forties understand Cajun because they heard it at home, they don't speak it well. Their children rarely heard the language spoken at home, so they grew up knowing even less.

Although traditional Cajun homes such as these have become rare, you can still see them scattered across southern Louisiana.

CAJUN HOUSES

The distinctive appearance of a traditional Cajun house makes it easy to recognize, even from a distance. One clue is the sharply peaked roof, which slopes straight down the front and back of the building. Under the roof, a long porch, or **galerie**, runs along the front of the house, supported by wooden posts. In the days before air-conditioning, it was often more comfortable to sit on the galerie than to go inside. This made the galerie a very popular place for spending time with friends and family.

Meghann's house, which is nestled among one hundred pine trees, is a newer version of the old Acadian style home.

Unlike most other houses, a traditional Cajun home is not built on a regular foundation. Instead, it sits above the ground on cement blocks. This protects the home from the frequent floods of southern Louisiana. The space under the house also creates breezes that help to cool the house in the hot, humid Louisiana weather.

But the thing that really sets a traditional Cajun house apart is the stairway on the front porch leading up to the attic. In years past, the attic was where the boys of the family slept. Since the French word for boy is **garçon,** this room was called the **garçonnière.** Having the stairs on the outside of the house was a good idea for several reasons. First, it kept the boys from tracking their muddy shoes through the main house. Putting the stairs on the outside also left more space in the room downstairs. And the steps of the stairway could be used as extra seats on the galerie.

From 1800 to the 1880s, almost all the homes on the Louisiana prairie were built in the Cajun manner. Then, new immigrant groups began to introduce other types of homes—styles that were often adopted by Cajuns as well. Since the traditional Cajun homes were built of wood, most eventually fell into disrepair and were replaced by more modern homes. Still, some of these newer houses have kept aspects of the old Cajun cottages.

Meghann's family lives in a modern version of the traditional Cajun home. Like an old-fashioned Cajun house, it is made of wood and raised above the ground on blocks. The roof slopes straight down from front to back, creating a porch on the main part of the house that is identical to an old-fashioned galerie. The only thing that is missing is an outdoor stairway to the attic.

Recently, people have been making an effort to change this. Instead of punishing children for speaking French, public schools like the ones Meghann and Jared attend are now teaching the language. However, since few teachers can speak Cajun French, the French that Meghann and Jared are learning is

Sugarcane is another crop grown in southern Louisiana. When the cane gets this high, it's ready to be harvested.

the modern French spoken in France and Canada. Still, most people are happy that the Cajun language is being respected again, and are pleased that their children are at least learning to speak some kind of French.

It is important to Alida and Moïse's parents that they learn Cajun, not standard French. So, every other week, they travel to Lafayette, the nearest big city, to take private lessons from a Cajun teacher. They practice by visiting family friends who speak Cajun, and by talking with their father, who grew up speaking Cajun. Their mother is learning along with them, although she had a head start—she could already speak standard French.

Meghann, Jared, and Alida all like speaking French. "It's hard," Jared says, "but every time you learn something new, you feel proud of yourself."

Alida's song is very popular with Cajun audiences.

"YOU WON'T COURT ME!"

Alida not only plays and sings songs, she writes them too. She wrote this half-joking, half-serious song to express her feeling that it's important for Cajun children to learn the Cajun language—not the French spoken in Paris.

It's fun to watch Alida and Moïse perform this song. She sings the words in Cajun and he translates them into English. But as a protective older brother, he manages to let the audience know he doesn't think anyone—even Cajun-speaking boys—should be dating his twelve-year-old sister.

Keep in mind that the words rhyme in Cajun, although they don't when they're translated into English. Also, the Cajun words are spelled phonetically—just as they would be spoken.

FIRST VERSE
Y'a juste ann affaire que mon je hais
    (There's just one thing I hate)
Les parleurs d'anglais dans mon pays.
    (English speakers in my country.)

CHORUS
Tee vas pas me courtiser, tee vas pas me courtiser,
    (You won't court me, you won't court me,)
Tee vas pas me courtiser, ormis tee parle francais.
    (You won't court me unless you speak French.)

SECOND VERSE
Oh, j'ai etez au bal pas longtemps passe
    (I went to the dance not so long ago,)
Tout les beau garcons peut pas parler francais.
    (All of the cute boys couldn't speak French.)

CHORUS REPEATS

THIRD VERSE
Parle-mon pas anglais, ni parisien.
    (Don't speak English or Parisian to me.)
J'veux atawnn seulement le vrai cadjin!
    (I only want to hear the real Cajun French!)

CHORUS REPEATS

Moïse's True Horror Story

Bayous make a great setting for spooky stories about evil beings like the jeck, a half monkey-half human creature who lures people to their deaths in the swamps. While the jeck may or may not really exist, some of the scary tales people tell are true. Moïse's story actually happened in the 1890s, when money was scarce and folks in the Louisiana prairies often had to do without most store-bought things.

"When my great-grandmother, Big Ma, was a little girl, they didn't have glass windows," he says. "It was too expensive. In Louisiana, it was warm enough most of the time to keep the shutters open and just put mosquito nets over the beds. The only time most people would pay to buy glass was for funerals.

"In those days, there was no embalming [treating the dead body to prevent decay], so they couldn't keep the coffin open at the wake, the way they do now. Instead, they had a glass window in the top of the coffin, so you could see the person's face.

"Well, at one point, an old farmer died and it was time for his wake. Back then, people used to sit up around the body all night long out of respect. So, they were sitting there next to him, and every now and then the glass would fog up on the inside. Since nobody had experience with glass in their houses, they didn't know what made it fog up. All night long, they'd lift up the lid, wipe the glass clean, and then close the lid again. Then, the next day, they buried him.

"Years later, they finally got glass windows around here. One winter, Big Ma was standing by the window, calling

50

one of her kids. It was cold outside, and every time she called, she breathed on the window and the glass fogged up. As she was wiping the glass off, she thought to herself, 'This is exactly what happened long ago at that wake.'

"Suddenly, it hit her why the glass in the coffin had fogged up. The man in the coffin must have been breathing on it. 'Oh, my lord!' she cried. 'We buried that man alive!'"

One thing that's never been in danger of dying out is the Cajuns' love of dancing. *Fais do-dos,* high-spirited community dances that include the whole family, have been popular for as long as there have been Cajuns in Louisiana, and they are still a great way to have fun! Unlike social dances in other parts of the country, everyone dances with everyone else at a fais do-do—children with their parents, grandparents, uncles, and cousins; girls with their sisters, brothers, and friends. Almost everyone in Eunice knows how to do the two-step and the waltz, the traditional dances at a fais do-do. Younger people also dance to **zydeco** and rock music.

There are plenty of opportunities to dance to Cajun music around Eunice, but one of the best places is the Liberty Center. Every Saturday night, people pack the auditorium at this theater to hear Cajun and zydeco bands and Cajun comics. Between the seats and the stage is a dance floor, and people get up and dance whenever they feel like it.

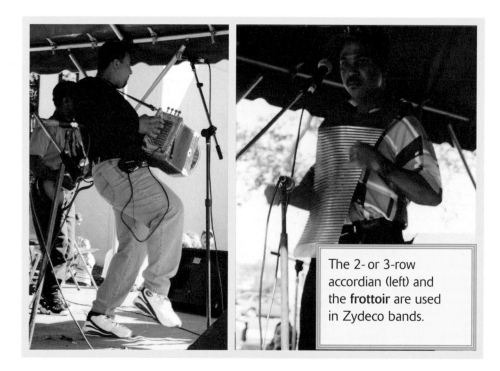

The 2- or 3-row accordian (left) and the **frottoir** are used in Zydeco bands.

ZYDECO

Zydeco is a close cousin of Cajun music and is very popular throughout southern Louisiana. It originated in the late 1940s when African-American musicians began to blend the light, springy rhythm of Cajun music with the sounds of blues and New Orleans jazz. Zydeco performers also moved away from the Cajun practice of singing in French and began using English with an occasional sprinkling of French phrases. Most zydeco songs are now sung in English, and the rollicking rhythm of zydeco is closer to rock and roll than Cajun music is.

You'll find accordions, guitars, a bass, and drums in both Cajun and zydeco bands. But Cajun bands always include a

Billboards at the door of the center announce coming attractions.
This week it's Alida and Moïse.

fiddle and sometimes a steel guitar, while modern zydeco
bands do not. However, zydeco bands have a special instrument called a frottoir, or a rub board. The frottoir originated
from the old-fashioned washboards that people used to scrub
their clothes when they washed them. By running something
metallic up and down the grooves, zydeco musicians discov-
ered a great rhythm instrument. Soon, they began to make
rub boards that were light enough to be hung from the musician's shoulders, and the modern frottoir was born.

While waiting to perform, Alida dances with her mother. Then it is her turn to be on stage.

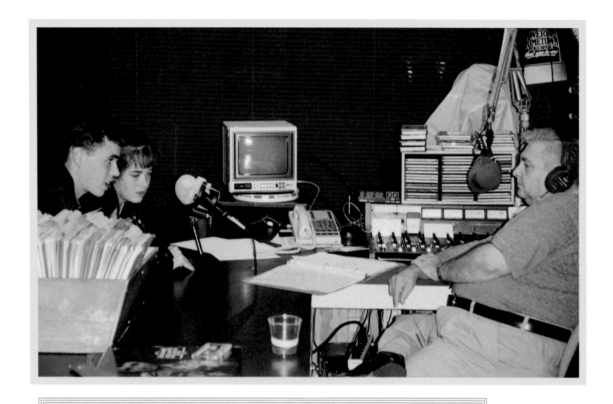

People in Eunice want to encourage pride in Cajun culture, so they're always happy to broadcast interviews with youngsters like Alida and Moïse.

A Cajun musician has to be very good to play at the Liberty Center. Linzay, Meghann's older brother, is an excellent fiddler and has performed there many times. Tonight, Alida and Moïse are among the performers scheduled. "We've played as far away as New Orleans and West Virginia," Alida says. "But I like playing at home best." Moïse agrees.

WASHING THE GRAVES

All Saints' Day, November 1, is an important religious event in French areas of Louisiana. This is the day when Catholics pray for those who have died. To mark All Saints' Day, the parish priest visits the cemeteries and blesses the graves.

"But before then," Meghann says, "you have to get everything ready for when the priest arrives. The church or whoever owns the cemetery cuts the grass. But as far as keeping the graves looking good, that's each family's responsibility."

Because underground water is very near the surface in southern Louisiana, graves are placed above ground, with cement or marble protecting the casket. The family makes sure that the cement covering is kept sparkling white. "We do that by whitewashing the graves every year," Meghann explains. "It's the families' job to do this. We buy whitewash powder in a bag and mix it with water. By All Saints' Day the graves are spruced up and have fresh flowers on them."

When Meghann's whitewash dries, the grave will be bright white.

The Saturday night performances are broadcast over the radio, so that people at home can enjoy the shows too. After they've finished playing, Alida and Moïse walk to the radio station and do a live interview. Then they go home to get some sleep.

Alida, Moïse, Meghann, and Jared are very proud of their hometown and their culture. Luckily, they—like other Cajuns—aren't likely to ever lose their love of dancing and listening to good music, eating great food, and having a good time. So it looks like the unique Cajun culture will be around for many years to come.

GLOSSARY

Bayou—A swampy river or stream in Louisiana. The word "bayou" comes from the Choctaw Indians.

Beau Fou (BO-FOO)—The Viators call their stud colt Beau Fou, or "Beautiful Fool."

Boucherie (BOOSH-ree)—A community butchering and cooking party.

Boudin (BOO-dan)—A highly seasoned Cajun sausage made of pork and rice.

Capuchons (KA-pee-shawn)—Pointed hats worn as part of the Mardi Gras costume.

Crackling—The crisp skin of roast pork.

Cuillères (KEY-YAIR)—Spoons. Cajun musicians hit two cuillères together to make a rhythmic sound.

Étouffée (AY-too-fay)—A Cajun stew served over rice.

Fais do-do (FAY-DO-do)—A neighborhood house dance.

Frottoir (Fro-TWAHR)—A corrugated washboard used as a percussion instrument in zydeco bands.

Galerie (GAHL-REE)—A long porch in the front of the house.

Garçon (Gahr-son)—A boy.

Garçonnière (Gahr-son-YAIR)—An attic bedroom for boys.

Gumbo—A thick, spicy soup thickened with okra. The name comes from an African word for okra.

Le 'tit fer (Luh-TEE-fair)—A triangle; one of the rhythm instruments in a Cajun band.

Levee—A dike made of earth.

58

Mardi Gras (MAH-de-grah)—"Fat Tuesday," one of the biggest Cajun holidays. Also refers to a person who celebrates the holiday.

Pistache (PEE-stahsh)—This is what Alida named her dog. It means peanut in Cajun French.

Zydeco (ZAH-dee-ko)—Snap beans, or zaricos, in French. The name of this type of southwestern Louisiana music was taken from a song with snap beans in the title.

Cypress "knees" are a familiar sight in the bayou.

MORE ABOUT CAJUNS

BOOKS

Picture Books

Cajun Night Before Christmas, by Trosclair (Pelican, 1101 Monroe St., Gretna, LA 70053, 1992).

> With an audio cassette narrated by Coleen Salley.

Jolie Blonde: A Cajun Twist to an Old Tale, by Sheila Hebert Collins (Blue Heron Press, PO Box 550, Thibodaux, LA 70302, 1993).

> Jolie, a Cajun goldilocks, visits her neighbors, the Heberts (pronounced "a bear"). The family is taking a *pirogue* (boat) ride while waiting for their gumbo to cool. This book includes a Cajun recipe and a list of the meanings and pronunciations of Cajun words. Both the author and the illustrator of this and the next book are from Cajun Louisiana.

Petite Rouge: A Cajun Twist to an Old Tale, by Sheila Hebert Collins, (Blue Heron Press, PO Box 550, Thibodaux, LA 70302, 1994).

> In this Cajun version, Little Red Riding Hood runs into the crafty alligator while crossing the swamp to bring *étouffée* to her grandmother. In addition to a dictionary and pronunciation guide, the book includes the author's family recipe for sauce piquante.

Cajun Alphabet, by James Rice (Pelican, 1101 Monroe St. Gretna, LA 70053, 1991).

> Not an ordinary ABC book, this alphabet book for older children uses poetry and color drawings to describe Cajun culture, life, and language.

Mardi Gras in the Country, by Mary Alice Fontenot (Pelican, 1101 Monroe St: Gretna, LA 70053, 1995).

> Marianne and Claude spend Mardi Gras at their grandmother's, whose house is one of the stops on the Mardi Gras run.

Mardi Gras: A Cajun Country Celebration by Diane Hoyt-Goldsmith (Holiday House, New York, 1995).

This book on Cajun Mardi Gras focuses on another family of musicians from Eunice. Color photos, recipes, and a song are included.

Short Novels

The Loup Garou, by Berthe Amos (Pelican, 1101 Monroe St. Gretna, LA 70053, 1979).

Set in 1755 in Nova Scotia, this is a story of a young Acadian boy and his family and their expulsion from French Acadie. The *loup garou* (a werewolf) and their Micmac Indian friends help Robert and his father escape from the British.

Poetry

Evangeline: A Tale of Acadie, by Henry Wadsworth Longfellow (Nimbus Publishing, Halifax, Nova Scotia).

One of the most famous American poems, *Evangeline* tells the story of a young Acadian girl and her fiancé, who were separated when the Acadians were deported.

History

Evangeline and the Acadians, by Robert Tallant (Random House: New York, 1957).

This interesting book traces the history of the Acadian people from their beginnings in Canada to the 1950s, when the book was written. The last chapter tells the story of Emmeline Labiche, the real-life Evangeline whose experience Longfellow used in creating his poem.

Magazine Articles

National Geographic, October 1990, "Cajuns Still Love Life."

This article discusses the history and present-day lifestyle of the Cajun people. It also includes some great photographs. The man pictured making boudin at the beginning of the article is Meghann's grandfather.

MUSIC ALBUMS

Cajun Music

The Balfa Brothers. *The Balfa Brothers Play Traditional Cajun Music.* Swallow Records, 1990.

Beausoleil. *Allons a Lafayette.* Arhoolie Records

Filé. *La Vie Marron: The Runaway Life.* Green Linnet, 1996.

Steve Riley and the Mamou Playboys. *Live!* (This album was recorded at a live performance in Eunice.) Rounder Records, 1994.

> The musician who first taught Alida to play the fiddle is the fiddle player here.

Zydeco Music
Clifton Chenier, King of the Bayous. *I'm Coming Home*. Arhoolie Records.

Keith Frank. *On the Bandstand*. Lanor Records.

Workshops
Cajun/Creole Week
Augusta Heritage Center
Davis and Elkins College
Elkins, West Virginia

> Those of you who would like to experience Cajun culture firsthand might enjoy the summer workshops and classes at the Augusta Heritage Center. Although this program focuses primarily on Appalachian folk culture, the center devotes a special week each year to Cajun music, dancing, cooking, history, and culture. Alida and Moïse have come here for the past two years to take fiddle and guitar lessons from famous Cajun musicians.

INDEX